Believe Me

why your **vision**, **brand** and **leadership** need a **bigger story**

MICHAEL MARGOLIS

a storytelling manifesto for change-makers and innovators

Book design by Erin Fitzsimmons
www.krop.com/efitz

Published 2009 by Get Storied Press
New York, NY

For information about bulk order special discounts
please contact Get Storied Press
www.believemethebook.com

PRINTED IN THE UNITED STATES OF AMERICA

First Edition: October 2009

ISBN 978-0-9842608-0-5

EARLY ENDORSEMENTS FOR **Believe** Me

"BELIEVE ME will help you become the leader you need to be. As futurist Rolf Jensen says, 'Storytellers will be the heroes of the 21st century.' This manifesto makes an inspired case for the future beyond just branding and the role of storytelling in the business equation."
Kevin Roberts, Worldwide CEO, Saatchi & Saatchi, and Author, *The Lovemarks Effect: Winning in the Consumer Revolution*

"Michael Margolis is a master of application. In this book he distills the richness of story as heritage and applies it to the heart of best business practices. May this handy guide open possibilities for more effective and memorable leadership in all who read it."
Christina Baldwin, Author of *Storycatcher: Making Sense of our Lives through the Power and Practice of Story, and The Circle Way: A Leader in Every Chair*

"In BELIEVE ME, Margolis describes the many factors reshaping the rules of business. If you want to excel as a leader of tomorrow, storytelling is a core thinking skill you can't afford to miss. This short little manifesto is an awesome and provocative addition to any business school curriculum."
Paul Dillon, Manager, Learning Strategies, Schulich Executive Education Centre, York University

"Stories drive innovation much better than spreadsheets or powerpoint ever will. BELIEVE ME provides a kaleidoscope view of storytelling and presents many possibilities for the crafting of future stories. Success has always been defined by how we weave stories into our brands and products."
Randy Voss, Senior Manager, Global Strategy and Business Development, Whirlpool Corporation

"For anyone committed to reshaping his or her own community, the starting place must be your own narrative. BELIEVE ME is an indispensible resource to start you on the journey."
Michael H. Shuman, Author, *The Small-Mart Revolution: How Local Businesses Are Beating the Global Competition*

"If you're selling a product—you're a salesman, which is perfectly fine. But, if you're selling an idea—there is usually something larger at stake. BELIEVE ME will elevate your vision and idea into action, especially

for the social entrepreneur with a story to tell. This book will take you there—believe me."
Robert Egger, Co-founder, Nonprofit Congress; President, DC Central Kitchen; and Author, *Begging for Change: The Dollars and Sense of Making Nonprofits Responsive, Efficient, and Rewarding for All*

"Reading the book BELIEVE ME offers you a guided tour through the world of your business, customers, or personal life in a way that makes existing stories pop out for you to see. Once you map the stories that exist, then your talent for storytelling, our 'most basic technology' will be spirited along with Margolis' guidance and suggestions."
Annette Simmons, Author, *The Story Factor and Whoever Tells the Best Story Wins*

"Powerful and easy to read. Margolis follows his own advice. He has told us the beginning of the story, led us into the middle, and entices us to write the ending. His provocative questions appear regularly throughout the book and serve as the light switch to turn on our storytelling."
Madelyn Blair, founder and President of Pelerei, Inc.

"Michael Margolis has done it again! Like a business storyteller's devotional, this concise and accessible work refreshed my understanding and commitment to better storytelling practice. It's authoritative, yet humble, paying due homage to others in the storytelling pantheon. It further comes with a great collection of resources and free bonuses—so the book easily pay for itself. If you liked Godin's *Tribes*, Zander's *The Art of Possibility* or Denning's *The Springboard*, you will enjoy this book."
Craig A. DeLarge, Associate Director, eMarketing & Relationship Marketing, Novo Nordisk Inc and Business Storytelling Strategist

"BELIEVE ME lights a blazing torch into new terrain of sense-making. Michael Margolis is a passionate and nimble guide. His manifesto serves as a map that every leader with a story will want as a companion. You will find nothing less than new sparks of innovation and organizational renewal in the process."
Terrence L. Gargiulo, President, makingstories.net, Author, *The Strategic Use of Stories in Organizational Communication and Learning*

"I love this book. Not only are the quotations profound, the axioms that follow them make you stop and think—about the stories you choose to tell and how you frame and craft them to achieve impact. I truly believe it'll shift the way you work with story in all aspects of your life."
Lori Silverman, Editor and Author, *Wake Me Up When the Data Is Over: How Organizations Use Stories to Drive Results*, **and Author,** *Stories Trainers Tell*

"At first glance, brand storytelling sounds so easy. And yet, after a closer look, you realize you're not telling anywhere near the best story—and that's the reason why your efforts are falling flat. This makes BELIEVE ME a very timely book—it's an inspired read that gets you thinking about stories with the proper frame of mind."
Aria Finger, Chief Marketing Officer, DoSomething.org

"This is such a timely book. Humanity is now more than ever yearning to be a part of a whole new story. BELIEVE ME reminds us that we are all co-authors of that new story. I believe this book not only convinces us of the power of story but challenges us to be mindful of how we tell our respective stories."
Victoria Wilding, CEO, SHIFT Foundation (Australia)

"Michael Margolis said it right: 'Only when people can locate themselves inside the story will they belong and participate in your narrative'. Right on cue, from the moment I started to read BELIEVE ME, I found myself following Michael's words and realized how much this short but powerful book was going to influence me, my organization and all our partners involved in social entrepreneurship. Margolis' bottom of page advice gave me plenty of practical ways to re-evaluate the power of my professional and personal narratives. I can't wait to re-read this manifesto and begin developing new and more effective stories."
Beverly Schwartz, Vice President, Global Marketing, Ashoka

"BELIEVE ME simply and elegantly illustrates why storytelling is the means to achieve our goals. We are reminded with compelling examples, strong axioms and vivid stories. I've been influenced and want more. A must read for anyone wanting to achieve, or to help others achieve success!"
Barbara Dammann, Executive Consultant, Enterprise Transformation, IBM Corporation

"For any change agent looking to get more people behind big and scary change, pay attention to BELIEVE ME's axiom Number Seven: 'If you want to change a culture, change the stories.' Powerpoint is not going to drive important change, but the right stories will. I hope many leaders read this book and follow the straight-forward advice that makes the case for deliberate storytelling as a core element of social change."
Kristen Grimm, founder of Spitfire Strategies and Author of *SmartChart 3.0* **and** *Activation Point*

"Are you facing skeptical consumers or constituents? If so, read this book. Michael Margolis is part of a new generation that understands the profound connection between inspired communication and social change. BELIEVE ME is a small book that packs a big punch and, in the process, challenges

V

lots of conventional thinking. It offers practical advice for calling upon the 'better angels' within your audience's true nature."
John Marshall Roberts, applied research psychologist, and Author, *Igniting Inspiration: A Persuasion Manual for Visionaries*

"We all love a good story. Here's how to tell them. Convincingly. Effectively. BELIEVE ME will challenge you to think differently about what makes a story work."
John Elkington, co-founder of SustainAbility, Volans Ventures, Environmental Data Services, and co-author of *The Power of Unreasonable People: How Social Entrepreneurs Create Markets That Change the World*

"For anyone trying to get their audience to own the story, read this book! BELIEVE ME reminds us that real lasting engagement requires a much, much bigger story. Margolis re-frames the conversation of social transformation in a very refreshing manner. It's useful for any leader doing something meaningful to create change in their organization or community."
Judy Braus, Senior Vice President of Education and Centers, National Audubon Society

"'How do you tell a story that others can find themselves a part of?' BELIEVE ME is a place to start and come back to in search of the answers within. Thank you, Michael, for preparing us so well for the journey!"
Cheryl Ka'uhane Lupenui, President and CEO, YWCA of O`ahu

"As a global health leader, I visit many countries, on many continents, each year. BELIEVE ME delivers a refreshing perspective on how international cooperation is defined by the stories we tell. The manifesto's anthropological slant delivers a modern remedy to the many cultural and economic divides that otherwise separate."
John P. Howe, III, M.D., President and CEO, Project HOPE

"Stories must be compelling, truthful, beautiful, believable, and inspirational if they are to have an impact on the lives of others. BELIEVE ME will remind you, as is it did me, how important these principles are in the stories we read and share. Outstanding!"
Bonnie Thorne, Senior Director of Development and Outreach, Center for Investigating Healthy Minds, University of Wisconsin-Madison

Believe in yourself. And stop trying to convince others.

—DE LA VEGA

NYC Street Artist/Philosopher

To the change-makers and innovators with the courage to swim in the deep end of the pool.

To my parents, each the revolutionary, who gave me freedom to look at the world with a fresh pair of eyes and reach beyond social conventions.

ACKNOWLEDGEMENTS

This book wouldn't exist without the generous guidance and support from countless colleagues, professionals, and friends.

First and foremost: Barbara Musser, Robbe Richman, and Francesca MacAaron, for being such creative partners and sounding boards as my voice came to life.

Erin Fitzsimmons for her remarkable book design and visual interpretation. Jamie Braughton for all the book publishing inside scoop and encouragement. Sam Rosen and Thoughtlead for the remarkable BELIEVE ME website and book promotional support. Erin Daly and Graham Van Dickhorn for helping me clarify the bigger picture. Michelle Levy for her editing and publishing insights. Lori Silverman for my first big break as a published author, and encouraging this next chapter.

Also thanks to many supportive colleagues who witnessed the process, including Robert Middleton, Stefan Doering, Joanne Goodrich, John Battaglia, Dan Lerner, Scott Milano, and Michelle James. You guys were my rock steadies through and through.

Lastly, to the story masters whose shoulders I proudly stand on: Paul Costello, Peter Block, Christina Baldwin, Seth Godin, Annette Simmons, Kevin Roberts, Steve Denning, Andy Goodman, Tom Peters, Robert Dickman, Seth Kahan, Patrick Hanlon, Robert McKee, and countless others who deserve mention. You've all informed the ideas I have distilled into this Storytelling Manifesto for Change-Makers.

TABLE OF CONTENTS

INTRODUCTION

If you are a visionary, innovator, or entrepreneur, this book is written with you in mind.

BELIEVE ME introduces a series of concepts for how to get others to believe in your story. You might be a change-agent inside your organization, or a visionary leader trying to improve society. It doesn't matter. The secret to persuasion, influence, and motivation is a formula deeply grounded in storytelling.

This might seem hard to believe at first blush. What do "once upon a time" fairy tales have to do with business and leadership results? You're right. I am not talking about bedtime stories or sitting around the corporate campfire. Yet, there is a reason why children love when you tell them a story. We are hardwired to seek and make sense of the world through narratives.

Anthropologists contend that 70 percent of everything we learn is through stories. Even as we grow into stubborn adults set in our ways, we fundamentally remain a storytelling species. This is just one of the reasons why 175,000 new blogs are started everyday. The real promise of technology and the Internet revolution is that everyone is now a storyteller. Finding real meaning and substance in our Twitter/Facebook chatter is another matter. Despite all the noise, in the words of Joan Didion, "We tell stories in order to live."

If you are trying to get others to see what you see (whatever your objective might be), you need to understand the fundamental role of storytelling. As a leader trying to influence and inspire others, you are measured on your ability to tell stories that make others care, believe, and act on what's most important.

My Path With Story

I first learned these lessons as an entrepreneur just out of university. It was 1998, and the New Economy was still finding its sea legs. I began working at the frontiers of social innovation—when the words "technology," "business," and "social change" in the same sentence drew mostly blank stares. The new frames of reference were still being invented.

As entrepreneurs we could feel something palpable in the air. The rules of the game were changing. Seminal books like Malcolm Gladwell's *The Tipping Point* and Seth Godin's *Unleashing The Idea Virus* were still two years away. Yet it was obvious that a new playing field was emerging. *Fast Company* magazine emerged to describe this new cultural phenomenon. Innovation, change, and entrepreneurship have since become the new "business as usual."

Two nonprofit start-ups later, I had achieved a fair amount of success while still in my early twenties. Funding from the Ford and Rockefeller Foundations, a profile in *Fast Company*, and invitations to speak across the country told me I was doing something right. In my case, I had become an unlikely evangelist for the Digital Divide—determined to tell the story of fundamental shifts that redrew the boundaries for economic success.

I was a proud participant in the first wave of social entrepreneurship—an evolving practice of applying business principles to social issues like poverty, education, and the environment. I was incubated by pioneers in the field, including, New Profit Inc., one of the first venture philanthropy funds to apply a business investor's mindset to the process of social change.

Yet, intuitively I knew something was missing from the conversation. It was the late '90s, and the way social innovation was typically framed by media or expert consultants didn't sit right with me. The first hurdles to address were old clichés about the poor and disenfranchised. Perhaps well-intentioned efforts at "doing good" perpetuated an imbalance of power. Social enterprise promoted a rational, "no-nonsense" business approach. Yet, attempts to make social change more quantifiable led to the larger story—the human story at the heart of everything—getting lost in translation. The spreadsheets were now running the asylum.

Several years later, I reinvented myself as a business storyteller. With a degree in cultural anthropology, I began to explore the broader implications of innovation and technology on our social and organizational habits. How does anything new or different make its way from the unfamiliar and foreign into mainstream acceptance?

My father is an inventor and my mother is an artist. So, I learned at an early age about creative freedom and the struggle to translate new ideas into something real for others. I eventually discovered the power of storytelling—as a cure for the pain I'd experienced trying to make my own ideas accessible to resistant guardians of the status quo.

How Ideas Become Reality

The quest for acceptance, "crossing the chasm" in the words of the great marketer Geoffrey Moore, is the essential course any visionary, innovator, or entrepreneur must take.

The value of narrative exists far beyond just an investor pitch, illustrative vignette, or inspired speech. The stories we choose literally make our world. Our identities, our beliefs, and our values all live and breathe in the matrix of stories. It's the *prima materia* of how we each perceive reality—our culture's collective agreements. A search for answers begins to show how the dots are connected. It is hard not to see the huge implications of storytelling in an increasingly brand-driven, and experience-based economy. It's all about the stories.

Consider your last visit to IKEA, Disneyworld, or the Apple store. You might have loved it, or been totally annoyed about the quality of service. Every experience is stored in the mind with a story attached to it. This means every brand is only as strong as the stories people tell about it. This explains why "word-of-mouth" is the new marketing Holy Grail. We only spread stories that are worth talking about—either the really bad stuff that upsets us, or the good stuff that lights up our day with an unexpected smile.

This little book is ambitious in that it explores how to "think in story"—how narratives are at the heart of all human experience. In just 88 pages, you will be introduced to the secret launch codes for effective visioning, branding, leadership, change, and innovation. If you learn how to change the story, you can change anything.

Engaging the Status Quo

In any given situation, a dominant story already exists. Who controls this story? It might be your biggest competitor, a recognized adversary, or the established social norm. You need to crack the existing code before you can socialize your own story into reality.

The trick is not to confront or challenge the status quo head-on. Rarely does anything productive emerge from gruesome hand-to-hand combat. And yet so many people trying to effect change or innovation prepare themselves for battle.

The moment you question and challenge someone else's beliefs, the debate is over—before it's even started. You must instead nurture and seduce your new story's acceptance. Do not judge or negate the established storylines. They have played an important role serving the social order. Perhaps, the old story has outgrown its utility or relevance, which is why your new story can find fertile ground. Just look for the cracks where new flowers can sprout and blossom.

Whatever constraints you perceive in the exisiting market are usually connected to the old story. Look for the bigger story—the more universal human story that cuts across old boundaries, limits, and categories. Break free from mental slavery and you've completely redefined the problem. With this shift in perspective, the solution is often much easier to achieve.

So whether you're launching a revolutionary business, rebuilding your community, or trying to teach the next generation, this book is an invitation into something larger. It will provide you with a fresh perspective on storytelling beyond simple anecdotes or adversarial politics. Are you brave enough to take, along with the axioms, a true leap of faith?

We have been trained, taught, and socialized to define everything in dualistic terms. Good/Bad, Real/Fake, Right/Wrong. Yet these sometimes useful labels separate us from the totality of human experience. Storytelling works best when you move beyond black and white, and start to explore the gray matter. Gray is the new black. Or is purple the new black? I can never keep it straight.

Finding Relevance

In a wildly adaptive world, the way we do business is evolving rapidly. We're all facing newfound freedoms of information, identity-formation, and innovation. Figuring out who you can trust is easier said than done. Which is why so many of us are suspicious of whatever we're being "sold" or told we should believe.

Most innovators know deep in their hearts that what they're trying to communicate would benefit humanity...if they could only get others to see, care, and believe in the same story. Somehow we're missing the core language we need to re-envision and re-invent this world. Storytelling is about making choices, and every choice reflects a deeper set of beliefs and values. Your choices have everything to do with how the story is received, accepted, or rejected by others. Can people belong and identify with your story?

You must learn how to meet others where they currently stand. People listen to stories naturally seeking to find beliefs and values that reinforce their own. You must simultaneously call people to a higher realm, and remind them of the bigger story so often taken for granted. The magic happens in this expanded place of possibility. You can ultimately help others shift their relationship with the world. This knowledge guides and informs your deepest desire—to get others to believe in you.

Understanding This Book's Format

This short manifesto is intentionally designed and attempts to embody the message of narrative. The format follows the classic three-act story structure: Set-up, Confrontation, and Resolution.

All three sections start with a timeless parable that informs the larger journey. Five short chapters then follow per section. Each chapter is a self-contained expression and lesson. It introduces a core axiom, and then provides you with useful context and illustration. Every chapter is anchored with a quote that reinforces the ubiquitous implications of storytelling.

You will undoubtedly recognize many of the luminaries quoted throughout the book— Barack Obama, Tom Peters, Gloria Steinem, Seth Godin, and Joseph Campbell, to name a few. I also feature many peers who I follow in the field of business storytelling. Many of the world's most successful leaders already embrace, prioritize and "think" in story.

While BELIEVE ME is sufficiently small to read in a single sitting, it's hopefully provocative enough to come back to again and again. Let the axioms be a touchstone as you work to bring your new visionary story into acceptance. You are encouraged to flip through and enjoy the book any way you choose.

You can easily read the manifesto straight through, cover-to-cover. You can also skip around or just read it two pages at a time. Each section, and furthermore each chapter, is designed to stand on its own. And yet the whole is greater than the sum of the parts. You may begin to see how the past, present, and future are inextricably linked. You might just need to go to the end of the story, in order to find your way back to the beginning.

This book serves as an introduction to why a story mindset is at the heart of all change and innovation. Forthcoming volumes will dive much deeper into the practical how-to steps for applying these principles to your work and life. I'm eager to provide you with in-depth action guides on: 1) what stories every entrepreneur must master, 2) how to use stories to effect large-scale change, and 3) the powerful elements that can transform any brand into a cultural flashpoint. My writing is informed by my ongoing teaching at the business school level, along with interactive workshops, hands-on consulting, and one-on-one coaching.

There are too many world-changing initiatives that fail because they don't tell a big enough story. Or at least a story big enough for people to project themselves into. It's my mission to help reframe this conversation.

I welcome your thoughts, feedback, and correspondence.

You can reach me at michael@believemethebook.com.

Metaphors be with you,

September 9, 2009

ACT I ›
How Ideas Become Reality

THE LONG WALK HOME

The Hero's Journey is one of our oldest stories.

As the great mythologist Joseph Campbell illustrated, this one story form is a basic archetypal myth that exists across every society and period of human history.

There's an important part to the Hero's Journey that often gets overlooked. It is, in my opinion, of the greatest significance to the innovator, change-maker, and visionary.

Let me remind you how the basic story goes...

We find the hero living an ordinary life. One day something happens that makes her somewhat uncomfortable. But she dismisses this feeling and goes back to her familiar pursuits. Signs continue to appear, until finally something pivotal tells her that she can no longer ignore the call to adventure.

So the hero gathers her courage, and leaves mostly everything else behind. She heads out of the village and into the wilderness. She doesn't yet know her destination, she just knows that she can no longer remain and accept the status quo. As she travels through the unknown, she unavoidably gets lost. And along the way, teachers appear and she learns new skills that build her confidence.

Eventually she makes her way to a mountain. Various tests and tribulations follow as she tries to make her way to the peak. Near the summit, she discovers a hidden, innermost cave. It is here she must face and slay the proverbial dragon. If she succeeds, she receives a great gift of gold, wisdom, and learning. If she fails, the journey is over at great loss to herself and humanity. With triumph, comes the moment of illumination, as she stands on the top of the world with great mysteries of the universe revealed.

And yet, the Hero's Journey does not end on top of the mountain. There is a second half to the story we often forget.

It's called the Long Walk Home. When the hero must make her way back down the mountain—into the valley where the river flows and things grow. She must navigate her way back to the village. Of course, she comes sprinting down the mountain, eager to share her newfound wisdom with the world. She can already imagine a hero's welcome—trumpets blaring, ticker-tape parade, a party in the streets...

And yet, when she finally makes her way home...

Nobody is standing at the gates to welcome her back. Nobody sent out the memo for the ticker-tape parade. Nobody brought the piñata and margaritas. It seems like folks didn't even care to notice she was gone. They're certainly not interested in listening to what she has to say *now*. Her attempts to connect with others are returned with blank stares of confusion and disbelief.

The Long Walk Home is the most heartbreaking part of many a Hero's Journey. Every visionary comes down the mountain with great gifts to serve humanity. Yet a painful experience of social rejection and disconnection usually follows. The hero simply seeks a triumphant return home. If she could only bottle the magic, others could drink from the well.

Perhaps you can relate to this mythic tale? BELIEVE ME offers a new storied pathway home—Cinco de Mayo party and all!

When you're conversing with coworkers, customers, or investors, the richness and meaning of your story is what people really buy.

Everybody thinks it's the return on investment that you're selling...but it's really the story about ROI that an investor takes away.

—TOM DUREL
former CIO/SVP, Blue Cross Blue Shield
and former CEO, Oceania

MEANING

People don't really buy a product, solution, or idea, they buy the story that's attached to it.

At their most basic, every hotel offers a bed, clean sheets; maybe a warm breakfast. But that's where similarities end. More than just higher thread count, most high-end hotels differentiate by "selling an experience." For a lesson in competing storylines, just look at the Las Vegas skyline, where each hotel provides a very different experience to choose from. This is a story that doesn't, as the saying goes, "just stay in Vegas..."

Humans are not plain, rational beings. We seek experiences that spark our imaginations and kindle the spirit. Stories are the pathway in.

Consumers want a story that goes beyond the mundane, and reminds them of what's bigger. The most innovative and memorable brands are rooted in this sacred knowledge— using the senses, mystery, and intrigue to give us something remarkable to remember.

50 years ago, market value was determined through sober means. Hard assets like your factories, inventory, and physical goods drove the balance sheet. Recent research from KPMG and Price Waterhouse estimates 60 percent or more of a company's value is now based on "intangibles." The brand, its people, processes, know-how, goodwill, and intellectual capital all work in tandem to create today's competitive advantage.

Stories are the most direct path to harnessing, managing, and communicating the value of your intangibles.

How do you measure or manage the "intangibles"? You either create sophisticated spreadsheets (trust me, people do), or you frame stories that communicate the bigger idea. Who would you rather be—a Mac or a PC?

Evaluate the value of your intangibles. What is most meaningful or memorable about your story? What kind of bigger experience might people pay a premium for?

5

PERCEPTION

A brand is far more than just a name, a logo, or a tagline; it's the stories that people tell about you.

I used to capture my ideas with a sea of Post-It notes. Until the day I discovered Moleskine notebooks with their distinguished round corners, ribbon bookmark, elastic closure, and expandable back pocket. More than just function or design, the brand's illustrious story is what I bought into. Resurrected from the brink of bankruptcy, Moleskine has since become a brand of choice across creative communities. These were the legendary notebooks preferred by Hemingway, Picasso, Van Gogh, and other prolific creatives. This was the tool they used to capture their ideas before finding their fame. Such epic origins speak to the dreamer in all of us.

A brand story is a symbolic container for the meaning of stuff.

In modern society, brands have become personal totems and value expressions for our lives—defining who we are, or who we aspire to be. As a passionate thinker and writer, Moleskine tells a story I readily buy into. It fits with my model of the world and how I want to see myself. Every brand (especially the successful, iconic one) communicates an enduring narrative—with advertising, packaging, and an experience that touches the imagination.

A brand story is more than just a static or definitive statement.

A brand's identity must evolve and change over time, just like a person does. This is why a brand story is never completely finished...it must always seek to invent the next chapter, without forgetting where it comes from. Every brand story needs a strong sense of origin, with a distinct point of view, and clear cultural contribution. These are your narrative anchors.

Develop a better sense of how your brand is perceived.
Where might you go and listen to stories about your brand?
What are the competing versions that you might hear?

A great brand is a story that's never completely told.

Stories create the emotional context people need to locate themselves in a larger experience.

—SCOTT BEDBURY

Author, **New Brand World: Eight Principles for Achieving Brand Leadership in the 21st Century**

I had to know and understand my own story before I could listen to and help other people with theirs.

—BARACK OBAMA
44th President of USA

RELATIONSHIP

Every story exists in relationship to everything else around it.

Our global crisis of confidence is rooted in stories that no longer work. No other time has shown a greater need for us to reexamine our relationships.

The way we think about the world is outdated. The way we think about our economy is outmoded. The way we think about our organizations is obsolete. We have the opportunity to "re-story" our relationships into something that makes more sense.

You can't really be in relationship with others if you don't know where you stand yourself. It's a core challenge of the visionary: to stand apart as an unconventional thinker—yet make your ideas accessible and acceptable to others.

There's much to learn from America's Storyteller-in-Chief.

Politics aside, President Barack Obama is a masterful storyteller. Using refined oratory and rhetoric skills, he clearly articulates where we stand in historical context—past, present, and future. Obama brilliantly uses his own personal story. For, his story *is* the American story—drawing on an enduring work ethic, the immigrant son achieves great strides. In hearing Obama's story, many see and recognize their own story.

Storytelling becomes an invitation into relationship.

As a visionary, you must come to peace with being the outsider. Stop trying to swim upstream or do battle with the establishment. Seduce your enemy with a story that speaks to all of humanity including those that might not typically agree.

Get really clear on what makes your story real and approachable.
What part of your own personal story must you reveal?
Where might you need to change the existing story?

MEMORY

We all want to look back at the story of our lives, and know that it made sense.

It's only human. We seek the invisible lines of connection. We must rationalize events in order to get our good night's sleep. Similarly, what ties a story together is causality: how one thing is related to the next, through a logical sequence of cause and effect. We're reasonable people, and we need it all to add up. Your audience requires and expects the same.

Scientists explain that our species is literally hardwired for storytelling.

Our perceptions, emotions, and relationships are all closely shaped by the narrative, sense-making process. We don't remember an exact experience, but instead produce a story that represents our interpretation or relationship to that event. Perhaps we seek experiences so that we have interesting stories to tell?

All scientists agree. Human memory is a narrative-driven process.

Quite simply, every experience, every relationship, every subject is stored in the mind with a story connected to it. The funny thing is that memory is not a static thing, or so the thinking goes from cognitive psychology.

Over time, our memories can be reframed to best align and reconcile with our current state of mind. Something once traumatic can eventually be transformed into a "growth experience," or equally remain as a tragedy that forever changed one's life for the worst.

Engage dynamically with the past, present, and future.
Where in time is your audience or customer stuck in the story?
How might you start to shift their view?

10

The ability to see our lives as stories rather than unrelated, random events increases the possibility for significant and purposeful action.

—DANIEL TAYLOR

Author, **Tell Me a Story:**
The Life-Shaping Power of Our Stories

Those who tell the stories
rule the world.

—HOPI AMERICAN INDIAN PROVERB
Also attributed to PLATO, Greek Philosopher

CHOICES

For a moment, consider all the stories that you inherited—from your family, school, religion, society, and others. How often do you question the validity of the stories you consume? Many of us accept stories implicitly, based on their "trusted" source of origin. Those who control or shape the larger collective story define the bounds of reality for others. We are so quick to judge other people's stories, yet we so unconsciously accept so many of our own.

Who should you trust to narrate your own story?

Much of our collective story is shaped and controlled by an elite few. Reality is a subjective choice, and there is no bigger power than framing the collective conversation. With great power comes great responsibility—which you must accept if you are to assume your own role as personal Chief Storyteller.

Storytelling is defined as much by exclusion as by what makes it to the "made for TV" version.

We've all struggled to get through a badly edited film. We've also seen great stories compromised and jeopardized when packaged for popular consumption. The big screen adaptation is rarely as good as the book, because there is much less room for nuance, complexity, and time to unfold the story. Boil it down to an elevator pitch and the pressure is on to cut to the chase.

Every story is the fine craft of editorial decisions. It's your job as storyteller to decide what part of the experience belongs on the cutting room floor—without losing the integrity of the message. What is most relevant? Your choices will invariably obscure as much as they reveal.

Examine the choices you've made with your story. Where are you reinforcing or challenging the status quo? What can you leave out to advance the story?

ACT II))
Engaging the
Status Quo

TRAVELING OFF THE MAP

Along the southern of coast of Portugal is a remote place that holds a special footnote in human history.

It's called Sagres Point (pronounced SAG-RESH). In bygone days, it was a sacred promontory dating back to Roman and earlier times. Later it was turned into a monastery and military school. For many centuries, the scraggly peninsula was considered the westernmost point of the inhabited world.

It was here, in the fifteenth century, that Prince Henry the Navigator established a School for Seafarers. Students came from far and wide for a chance to study and prove their worthiness. Through apprenticeship and monastic devotion, students learned the arts of mapmaking, stargazing, and ocean navigation. They pioneered engineering that allowed ships to travel farther and faster than ever imagined. They learned how to listen to the sky and talk with the sea.

Nobody knew what fate awaited those who traveled off the map. Standing on the edge of the familiar, these brave initiates found the courage to move beyond what was previously known or thought possible. The established conventions of the day claimed the world fell off into oblivion out beyond the horizon. Travel into uncharted territory at your own peril.

While Prince Henry's school lasted barely 40 years, it left a timeless mark on global culture.

16

The European "Age of Exploration" took root at Sagres Point. Portugal soon dominated the seas for centuries, opening up trade routes between East and West and setting the stage for modern globalization. By 1571, the Portuguese Empire stretched across South America, Africa, India, and Southeast Asia.

Prince Henry even inspired a fellow Portuguese countryman, a certain Christopher Columbus, to venture west on a series of historic journeys. A brave new world is what he accidentally "discovered." What if they had not dared to travel beyond the status quo?

Today, we sense a new age of discovery just waiting beyond the horizon of what we currently see.

Institutions are increasingly being asked to navigate off the map. The old rules of the game are obsolete. This climate requires new thinking, new tools, and new approaches. Most importantly, it requires a new language—because you can't envision, much less communicate, new possibilities without the language to do so. Narrative provides your with a new vocabulary to navigate the convergence of realities.

History needs its brave visionaries and innovators. Especially at an important time like now. Our greatest collective leaps are made by those who brave to "think different." If you're reading this, you're likely the kind of person who's comfortable navigating the creative unknown.

But moving beyond the status quo to see the bigger story is a bigger nut to crack. You must learn how to translate what you see into a story others can equally believe. Confrontation is not the answer. When you cultivate trust and confidence, others will be willing to follow you into the new and unfamiliar. What stands in the way?

People don't want more information. They are up to their eyeballs in information.

They want faith—faith in you, your goals, your success, in the story you tell...

Once people make your story their story, you have tapped into the powerful force of faith.

—ANNETTE SIMMONS

Author, **The Story Factor: Inspiration, Influence, and Persuasion Through the Art of Storytelling**

DISBELIEF

The power of your story grows exponentially as more and more people accept your story as their truth.

After being told so many tall tales and empty promises, from politicians to marketers, it's easy to feel suspicious. People need a good reason to believe. They must self-identify within your story before they can commit to fulfilling its promise.

Stories reflect collective agreements about reality.

A story feeds on belief. The more deeply and widely it's believed, the more it becomes true. This could be belief in a specific God, or recognition that cigarettes kill. It was once believed the sun revolved around the earth, and slavery was the accepted norm. What's a widely held belief you need to confront?

Only when people can locate themselves inside the story will they truly belong and participate in your narrative.

This is why the global warming movement struggles to make greater impact. Granted, its now generally accepted as fact. But what is the average citizen doing about the issue? How are major nations really committing to solving the crisis?

While we can all intellectualize the problem, most of us have yet to experience a dramatic and direct consequence of the problem. Self-interest continues to trump collective action. "The Inconvenient Truth" tries to guilt and score us into action. Instead, we find ourselves scared, depressed, and powerless. A new story approach is required.

Choose a story angle that helps people get inspired and internalize the truth.
Why have people given up hope?
What can people agree on despite the differences?

CULTURE

**If you want to learn about a culture, listen to the stories.
If you want to change a culture, change the stories.**

Culture is the invisible fabric of our lives. It provides a set of social norms and assumptions that inform accepted behavior. Cultural values are often programmed through a set of stories and rituals that reinforce social order. In America, we have the myths of the cowboy, the puritan, and the maverick entrepreneur to fuel our collective ethos.

If you want to change how people think or behave, work within the stories that define that specific culture.

Culture guides us in knowing what is acceptable or not, within a specific social group. The very limits of what is real, what is good, and what is possible are defined in the boundaries of a cultural group's stories. What are your culture's stories?

Sometimes the greatest gifts of a culture lead to its stagnation.

We all know of NASA's epic scientific accomplishments. Like putting a man on the moon at a time when it sounded like science fiction. NASA succeeded with a simple cultural mantra of "failure is not an option."

And yet, decades later, after two space shuttle disasters, NASA lost its way. An investigation concluded the very same value that informed success ("failure is not an option") also created an environment where the open flow of information was not possible. The fear of failure meant people were afraid to speak up despite obvious warning signs leading to catastrophe. A culture's stories, even stories of strength, come with inherent vulnerability.

Culture lives in its stories. Start listening.
What is the influence of culture on the story you're trying to tell?
What cultural values either support or stand in the way?

Culture is not about what is absolute, real, or true. It's about what a group of people get together and agree to believe.

Culture can be healthy or toxic, nurturing or murderous. Culture is made of stories...

—THOM HARTMANN
Author, **The Last Hours of Ancient Sunlight: Waking Up to Personal and Global Transformation**

21

The marketplace is demanding that we burn the policy manuals and knock off the incessant memo writing; there's just no time.

It also demands we empower everyone to constantly take initiatives. It turns out stories are a—if not the—leadership answer to both issues.

—TOM PETERS
Author, **Re-imagine! Business Excellence in a Disruptive Age**

LEADERSHIP

Leaders lead by telling stories that give others permission to lead, not follow.

The ultimate act of leadership is learning how to get out of the way. Of course, you need to first help others find their bearings. Too often, leaders present an innovation or change story that is profoundly incomprehensible to the people expected to implement it.

Clarity and alignment are necessary before you can possibly expect commitment. Only then can you trust people to make the right decisions in support of the collective dream.

Confidence in our leaders is based on their ability to live the story.

Messages from management are typically interpreted with suspicion. Remember, people have to believe in the story in order to belong to the story. It begins with your own personal story as the messenger. What is your credibility for leading us through the journey ahead? How do you model or demonstrate that story in your own daily actions? These are the criteria of evaluation that allow people to trust and embrace your story.

Real leaders know that they are NOT the story.

Despite appearances, Steve Jobs is not the story of Apple. He is the wisdom-keeper who keeps Apple true to its origin story—the mission to think different, and to make technology more human. Jobs has evangelized a culture that values intuitive design and emotional appeal. It permeates everything Apple does and became a core element of the company's DNA and continued success.

Look for ways to orient others into your story.
What ideas or experiences can give them confidence to follow your lead?
What would empower and allow people to lead for themselves?

23

CONVERGENCE

Storytelling is our most basic technology, evolved through twenty-first-century innovation.

Whether you're trying to Twitter, Facebook, or YouTube your way into popular consciousness, storytelling is still at the core of all effective communications. Even through the clutter of technology, we remain enraptured by the flickering flame of a good story.

We are fast approaching a tipping point in storytelling. The means of story production have been democratized.

If you have a story to tell, the Internet provides unlimited, affordable, and easy platforms for sharing your story with the world. Of course, if you want to get people's attention, you better have a really good story to tell. Technology is just the means, not the end in itself. The story is what's really at stake.

Technology has reshaped how information travels, both for the better and for the worse. It means your story can move at light-speed and be heard by millions around the planet. The media half-life for that exact same story can also last little longer than the blink of an eye.

Everybody has a story to tell. And everybody wants to tell it.

Identity and achievement is increasingly measured by one's personal story production. Whether you're channeling your inner artist or nurturing an entrepreneurial drive, your success is defined by your ability to tell the story. Just witness the explosion of social media, popular culture, and publishing. Technology provides the tools for sharing your ideas. Everybody wants to be a "somebody"—and that begins with having a story to tell.

Use technology to advance your story.
How is social media changing the process of storytelling?
What would get others wanting to spread your story?

Humans have been storytelling for 100,000 years around the campfire; the media is now our campfire.

—GLORIA STEINEM
Feminist icon, journalist, and activist
(Retweet from @randomdeann)

If you're going to have a story,
have a big story, or none at all.

—JOSEPH CAMPBELL
Mythologist

EPIC

There's a reason why we love larger-than-life heroic tales. Our spirit instinctively seeks to move beyond limitation. Our natural wonder as a child never disappears. We're constantly trying to re-live this feeling, despite the constraints and responsibilites that come with adulthood. We continue to seek stories that expand our understanding of what's possible. We feed this habit through never ending consumption of action movies, mystery novels, and shoot-em-up video games where we get to play make-believe.

There's no greater feeling than being the hero in your own story.

Modern advertising usually puts the consumer at the center of the story. Whether it's a Swiffer Duster or a Nissan Pathfinder, most products are sold through the same variation a on a dream—freedom, autonomy, control. Become the master of your own destiny: chart your own course.

If you're not selling a product or service, but trying to create broad scale change—it becomes insanely more complicated. You usually have more than just a single "customer." Instead, you're managing a range of stakeholders who all need to find their place inside the story.

Moving beyond constraints simply demands a bigger story.

Small stories offer little room to move. They feel confining and restrictive. Instead, look for the universal theme that anyone can get behind—a core value or human aspiration that's easy to connect with. The bigger the story, the more room under the tent for people to show up.

Look for places to expand the story.
How might you make your audience the hero in your story?
What might their actions do to transform the plot?

27

ACT III)))
Finding Relevance

RECLAIM WHAT WAS FORGOTTEN

A wise man and shopkeeper by the name Mohammad Bawa taught me the following story. It teaches an Akan West African value and proverb that reminds us "to go back and get it." Even as we move toward our future, we remain intimately dependent on our understanding of the past.

Sankofa

"Se wo were fi-na wo-sankofa a, yenkyi."

("It is not wrong to go back for that which you have forgotten.")

As the story of initiation goes, a warrior is floating down a river in a dugout canoe. It is only when he discovers heavy rapids ahead that he realizes his great oversight and quickly turns around.

The waters appeared calm when he first climbed into the canoe, so he chose to discard his wooden walking stick to lighten his load. Now he realizes the same long walking stick would be critical to a safe passage across water. He needs the stick to steer around heavy rocks that would otherwise crush his canoe. He has no choice but to turn around and retrieve what he previously tossed aside, thinking it was no longer needed.

In Adinkra symbols, Sankofa is often depicted as a mythical bird that flies forward while its head looks backwards. It represents the collective cycle of life and how our future is intimately tied to our relationship with the past.

What if storytelling is our collective Sankofa?

Sankofa invites us to go back and reclaim the essence of our humanity—our ability to communicate and connect through the stories we tell.

Even further, the proverb reminds us of our species' adaptive ability to imagine new possibilities—to see and create a new future. We cannot forget nor dismiss the past in the process.

There are countless institutions that we have already built that serve as the pillars of our society. Many now require reinvention, revitalization, and renewal. Not destruction or rejection.

We must reinvent our words to better reflect the world we seek to create. This can be achieved through a reconciliation of stories, from across our past, present, and future.

We must first envision the new future, and then use the past to legitimize this future. Instead of a story that emphasizes radical change and upheaval, we must seek the invisible lines of connection that reinforce coherence and stability.

Like the Sankofa bird, we must continue to fly forward, yet we without loosing our sense of the past. We just need to reframe our relationship with the past.

The seeds of our future were planted a long time ago for us to reclaim. You just need to know what part of the story needs to be retrieved. In the process you open the door to true reinvention.

Great stories agree with our world view. The best stories don't teach people anything new.

Instead, the best stories agree with what the audience already believes and makes the members of the audience feel smart and secure when reminded how right they were in the first place.

—SETH GODIN
Author, **Tribes: We Need You to Lead Us**

CHANGE

Nobody likes a change story, especially a change story we have no control over. What people really need is a continuity story.

We surround ourselves with stories that support our mental and emotional status quo. That's why if you're a hardcore liberal, it's difficult to listen to conservative shock-jocks like Rush Limbaugh. The same applies to FOX News die-hards who struggle with the liberal media conspiracy. We're always searching for stories that reinforce our view of how we see things.

Your story needs to speak to your audience's hearts, interests, and worldview.

You cannot guilt them, condemn them, or shame them. You need to articulate why your audience should care about the story you are trying to tell. Telling people they're wrong never gets you anywhere. It simply sets up adversarial conflict. Ghandi, Martin Luther King, and the Dalai Lama embody this message. Their work does not vilify or denigrate their adversaries. Instead they appeal to our greater humanity.

You can't change a story about something you hate or dislike.

Anything you push away will only push back harder. In the act of pushing it away, you are negating its very existence. It's a basic law of cause and effect. You can't really be in relationship with anything you want to get rid of. Whether you're trying to lose 15 pounds, or campaigning against a larger injustice, the same rules apply. Granted, you might be working in a broken system—but your new story must try to transcend divisiveness and connect with something universal.

Find something everyone can agree on. Build your story around this message.
Where can you make peace with your enemy?
What new possibilities might then emerge?

33

IDENTITY

The stories of identity are the foundation for everything else. Today, this can be summed up in a Facebook page. We seek stories in order to know who we are and where we belong.

We are completely lost without "stories" to orient where we are. Much of our lives are spent searching for a bigger story, our legend—a larger reason for being. And yet, as humans we easily become attached, if not enslaved, to these very same stories. The weight of stories can keep us trapped and suffering, unable to shift our relationships to the past, present, and future.

Stories are NOT the truth.

They are merely a projection of our interpretation of an experience, event, or person at any given time. Our relationship to the biography of our life story can change. Anybody who's ever made a huge and dramatic leap knows how flexible and adaptive their story can be. Just ask Martha Stewart.

I story, therefore I am.

Stories remain the invisible glue through which people narrate the meaning of their lives and interweave their lives with others lives. Where there is energy for a story to be told, there is karma to be experienced and released. Talk to any mystic or sage, and they will teach you how to move beyond "a fixed story" of your life. But the journey begins and can only be completed by recognizing where you are trapped in the current story. The same applies to larger social systems.

34

Consider your personal identity or tribe's identity. What part of the story no longer serves? How is the story held hostage or constrained?

There is no greater burden than carrying an untold story.

—MAYA ANGELOU

Poet Laureate

Storytelling reveals meaning without committing the error of defining it.

—HANNAH ARENDT

German Political Theorist

FREEDOM

Storytelling empowers, because it escapes the need to claim absolute truth.

Your audience always holds the flexibility to interpret and relate to your story as they so choose. And therein lies storytelling's expansive and redemptive freedom. Your story needs to be relevant in order to spread.

As a storyteller, you are forever at the mercy of your audience.

This makes storytelling the most accountable form of communication at our disposal. The narrative form is the great emancipator for evolutionary times. It's the ultimate relationship framework because it returns the balance of power and puts the burden of proof on the storyteller (often one who holds a position of influence).

Story by definition is a two-way communication medium.

You cannot craft and produce your story of innovation in isolation. Many of the world's greatest companies now employ customer panels and user communities to engage their audience in the product design process. Intuit (makers of Quicken and Quickbooks accounting software) uses anthropologists to better understand the evolving needs of customers. Using ethnographic research, Intuit doesn't literally ask customers their wants, but instead observes customers using the products in their natural environment.

The local unions of NYC employ a similar approach, enrolling Mayor Bloomberg and other top officials to spend one morning a month shadowing the life of a common constituent, from sharing breakfast at the kitchen table to riding the subway together. There's no better way to get real, than to walk in another's shoes.

Frame a story that reflects the reality of people's lives.
How might you learn about your customers' identity or lifestyle?
Where might you go to simply observe and listen?

EVOLUTION

Reinvention is the new storyline.

It seems people everywhere are reframing, reimagining, and reshaping their story. Whether its individuals, organizations, or society—these times call for dramatic re-invention. Remember that while you're preaching innovation, most people are still stuck in the old story's psychic and mental impressions.

Every story's evolution needs connection to history. The present and the future are meaningless without a direct correlation to the past.

As you introduce a new story vision, you must demonstrate its natural evolution. As the saying goes, "the victors write the history books." This is how nation-states invented traditions that enabled nationalism to trump tribalism in the sixteenth and seventeenth centuries. And it's how any brand creates a back story that customers, members, or donors can more easily buy into.

Introducing a new story without a clear contextual beginning, middle, and end is a recipe for disaster. Your audience will experience emotional dissonance unless you can offer the logical stepping stones for them to find their way into the new story. The Walmart brand recently evolved beyond just value to also 'living better'. Some connect with the new positioning while others find it rings hollow.

Storytelling is how we create trusted connections.

Five thousand years ago in Sumeria, merchants introduced seals of quality to distinguish their brands. This allowed trade relationships to evolve beyond neighbors to the farthest reaches of the globe. The same principles of perception are at play today, hyper-realized through new tools of web-based commerce and communications. If you want people to trust you and accept your invitation into relationship, you need a *believable story*.

Identify your natural sources of authenticity. What have you always done that reinforces your clear legitimacy? How can you maintain trust while in the midst of change?

It's all a question of story. We are in trouble just now because we do not have a good story.

We are in between stories. The old story, the account of how the world came to be and how we fit into it, is no longer effective.

Yet we have not learned the new story.

—THOMAS BERRY
Theologian, Philosopher, and Cultural Historian

Those who do not have power over the story that dominates their lives

—the power to retell it, rethink it, deconstruct it, joke about it, and change it as times change—

truly are powerless, because they cannot think new thoughts.

—SALMAN RUSHDIE
Novelist

PROPHESY

Storytelling is like fortune-telling. The act of choosing a certain story determines the probability of future outcomes.

Every culture and civilization flounders or flourishes based on its ability to tell relevant stories. We face an era of information overload and attention deficit. Information is increasingly free, and therefore diminishing in value—unless infused with true meaning. Computers work great with numbers, but they can't manage the meaning-making process. That's where humans, and our ability to narrate, control the fates.

Our general understanding of Darwin's theory is often mixed-up.

Bigger, stronger, faster is not necessarily better. Survival of the fittest is a lesson in adaptability. How well does any species respond to changing conditions? In our case, both physical limitations and pressures in our mental environment determine our coping skills. To adapt one's thinking, identity, and consciousness is the ultimate act of storytelling.

We cannot force our beliefs onto anyone. We must create a story worth believing. The future rests in our ability to tell these kinds of stories.

We are increasingly paid and rewarded in the marketplace for our ability to make meaning—whether that's telling a story about the balance sheet, or telling a story that inspires and motivates others. If we want to see a story take root and travel, we must nurture a new form of story intelligence. If we have the power to shape our destiny, then perhaps storytelling represents the path for our redemption.

Look to where people over-rationalize the story to death.
Where can you reframe what is or isn't possible?
What's the bigger story?

EPILOGUE

THIS STORY IS JUST BEGINNING

BELIEVE ME represents the rst of several books already in the works. The intent of this manifesto is to share the dream of a boundless blue sky and introduce you to the possibilities of how storytelling can reinvent our world.

Follow-up books will be more practical, with frameworks, case studies, and a how-to driven approach. I am eager to explore more deeply the topics of 1) brand storytelling, 2) social innovation stories, and 3) the stories every entrepreneur must tell.

The last page of this book outlines a series of Free Bonuses you can take advantage of right now. They will get you thinking more about how to apply BELIEVE ME's 15 storytelling axioms to your work.

For those who seek more hands-on learning, I offer one-on-one coaching programs designed to raise your Story Mojo. In Winter 2010, I am launching High-Stakes Storytelling, a six-month executive education program. This program provides a structured, intensive, action-based curriculum where you can directly apply time-tested concepts to a high-stakes story you're expected to deliver on. Visit www.getstoried.com to learn more.

The following Epilogue includes a bibliography of books referenced in BELIEVE ME. You can visit www.believemethebook.com for short reviews and easy access to each book.

Lastly, the Epilogue contains just a few more of my favorite quotes on storytelling. While the following quotes didn't make it into the main three acts, they remain a source of insight and inspiration. What axioms do you think match these additional quotes?

 What more about story do you want to learn or know?
Email me at Michael@believemethebook.com and our dialogue will form the basis of a blog and continuing discussion at www.believemethebook.com.

15 STORYTELLING

1. People don't really buy a product, service, or idea, they buy the story that's attached to it.

2. Your brand is far more than just a name, a logo, or a tagline; it's the stories that people tell about you.

3. Every story exists in relationship to everything else around it.

4. We all want to look back at the story of our lives, and know that it made sense.

5. The stories we tell literally make our world.

6. The power of your story grows exponentially as more and more people accept your story as their truth.

7. If you want to learn about a culture, listen to the stories. If you want to change a culture, change the stories.

8. Leaders lead by telling stories that give others permission to lead, not follow.

AXIOMS REVISITED

9. Storytelling is our most basic technology, turbo-charged through twenty-first century innovation.

10. We all seek to experience our life in the most heroic of terms.

11. Nobody likes a change story, especially a change story we have no control over. What people really need is a continuity story.

12. Our fate as a species is contained in the story. Both tyranny and freedom are constructed through well-supported narratives.

13. Storytelling empowers, because it escapes the need to claim absolute truth.

14. Reinvention is the new storyline.

15. Storytelling is like fortune-telling. The act of choosing a certain story determines the probability of future outcomes.

PUTTING IDEAS INTO PRACTICE

Here's a recap of the recommended next steps found at the end of each 15 chapters with the prompts and questions to explore in your story.

1. MEANING
Evaluate the value of your intangibles.

What is most meaningful or memorable about your story?

What kind of bigger experience might people pay a premium for?

2. PERCEPTION
Develop a better sense of how your brand is perceived.

Where might you go listen to stories about your brand?

What are the competing versions that you might hear?

3. RELATIONSHIP
Get really clear on what makes your story real and approachable.

What part of your own personal story must you reveal?

Where might you need to change the existing story?

4. MEMORY
Engage dynamically with the past, present, and future.

Where in time is your audience or customer stuck in their story?

How might you start to shift their view?

5. CHOICES
Examine the choices you've made with your story.

Where are you reinforcing or challenging the status quo?

What can you leave out to advance the story?

6. DISBELIEF
Choose a story angle that helps people get inspired and internalize the truth.

Why have people given up hope?

What can people agree on despite the differences?

7. CULTURE
Culture lives in the stories. Start listening.

What is the influence of culture on the story you're trying to tell?

What cultural values either support or stand in the way?

8. LEADERSHIP
Look for ways to orient others into your story.

What ideas or experiences can give them confidence to follow your lead?

What would empower and allow people to lead for themselves?

9. CONVERGENCE
Use technology to advance your story.

How is social media changing the process of storytelling?

What would get others wanting to spread your story?

10. EPIC
Look for places to expand the story.

How might you make your audience the hero in your story?

What might their actions do to transform the plot?

11. CHANGE

Find something everyone can agree on. Build your story around this message.

Where can you make peace with your enemy?

What new possibilities might then emerge?

12. IDENTITY

Consider your personal identity or tribe's identity.

What part of the story no longer serves?

How is the story held hostage or constrained?

13. FREEDOM

Frame a story that reflects the reality of people's lives.

How might you learn about your customers' identity or lifestyle?

Where might you go to simply listen and observe?

14. EVOLUTION

Identify your natural sources of authenticity.

What have you always done that reinforces your clear legitimacy?

How can you maintain trust while in the midst of change?

15. PROPHESY

Look to where people over-rationalize the story to death.

Where can you reframe what is or isn't possible?

What's the bigger story?

7 BONUS QUOTES

One of the most important things to keep in mind in using stories in organizations is to get clear, and stay clear, on the purpose for which the story is being used.

Because we human beings find stories such fascinating things, it is all too easy to get interested in the story for its own sake, and lose sight of the purpose for which we set out to use the story.

—STEVE DENNING

Author,

The Leader's Guide to Storytelling

The highest-paid person in the first half of this century will be the storyteller.

All professionals, including advertisers, teachers, entrepreneurs, politicians, athletes and religious leaders, will be valued for their ability to create stories that will captivate their audiences.

—ROLF JENSEN

Former Director of the Copenhagen Institute for Future Studies

The 'true' story is not the one that exists in my mind...The story in my mind is nothing but a hope; the text of the story is the tool I created in order to try to make that hope a reality.

The story itself, the true story, is the one that the audience members create in their minds, guided and shaped by my text, but then transformed, elucidated, expanded, edited, and clarified by their own experience, their own desires, their own hopes and fears.

—ORSON SCOTT CARD
American Science Fiction Writer

We have to have a version of our own story that we keep telling ourselves that allows us to get up in the morning.

This version of yourself is what you sell to yourself. I think it necessarily includes...not looking at certain things. Everybody's got some blind spot.

—STEVEN SODERBERGH
Academy-Award Winning Film Director

By refusing to have our stories bounded by race, belief, ideology, nationality, and even by time, and by grounding them in our awe of the universe, we choose to enact a larger, more hopeful and more positive story of humanity.

—MICHAEL BOGDANFFY-KRIEGH
Architect and Past President,
New York Society for Ethical Culture

We live in story like a fish lives in water. We swim through words and images siphoning story through our minds the way a fish siphons water through its gills.

We cannot think without language, we cannot process experience without story.

—CHRISTINA BALDWIN

Author, **Storycatcher: Making Sense of our Lives through the Power and Practice of Story**

What happens is fact, not truth.
Truth is what we think about
what happens.

—ROBERT MCKEE

Author, **Story: Substance, Structure, Style, and the
Principles of Screenwriting**

BIBLIOGRAPHY

There are several books referenced throughout BELIEVE ME.

Baldwin, Christina. *Storycatcher: Making Sense of Our Lives Through the Power and Practice of Story.* New World Library, 2007.

Bedbury, Scott. *New Brand World: Eight Principles for Achieving Brand Leadership in the Twenty-First Century.* Penguin, 2003.

Denning, Steve. *The Leader's Guide to Storytelling: Mastering the Art and Discipline of Business Narrative.* Jossey-Bass, 2005.

Godin, Seth. *Tribes: We Need You to Lead Us.* Portfolio Hardover, 2008.

Hartmann, Thom. *The Last Hours of Ancient Sunlight: Waking Up to Personal and Global Transformation.* Three Rivers Press, 2000.

Jensen, Rolf. *Dream Society: How the Coming Shift from Information to Imagination Will Transform Your Business.* McGraw-Hill, 2001.

McKee, Robert. *Story: Substance, Structure, Style, and the Principles of Screenwriting.* It Books, 1997.

Taylor, Daniel. *Tell Me a Story: The Life-Shaping Power of Our Stories.* Bog Walk Press, 2001.

Simmons, Annette. *Whoever Tells the Best Story Wins: How to Use Your Own Stories to Communicate with Power and Impact.* AMACOM, 2007.

Here are additional books related to the topics and ideas explored in BELIEVE ME.

Bhargava, Rohit. *Personality Not Included: Why Companies Lose Their Authenticity and How Great Brands Get It Back.* McGraw-Hill, 2008.

Dickman, Robert. *The Elements of Persuasion: Use Storytelling to Pitch Better, Sell Faster, and Win More Business.* Collins Business, 2007.

Fog. Klaus. *Storytelling: Branding in Practice.* Springer, 2005.

Godin, Seth. *All Marketers Are Liars: The Power of Telling Authentic Stories in a Low-Trust World.* Portfolio Hardcover, 2005.

Hanlon, Patrick. *Primal Branding: Creating Zealots for Your Brand, Your Company, Your Future.* Simon and Schuster, 2006.

Heath, Chip and Dan. *Made to Stick: Why Some Ideas Survive and Others Die.* Random House, 2007.

Lindstrom, Martin. *Buyology: Truth and Lies About Why We Buy.* Broadway Business, 2008.

Kleiner, Art. *The Age of Heretics: A History of Radical Thinkers Who Reinvented Corporate Management.* Doubleday Business, 1998.

Pearson, Carol. *The Hero and The Outlaw: Building Extraordinary Brands Through the Power of Archetypes.* McGraw-Hill, 2001.

Pine, B. Joseph, and Gilmore, James. *The Experience Economy: Work is Theatre and Every Business a Stage.* Harvard Business Press, 1999.

Roberts, Kevin. *LoveMarks: The Future Beyond Brands.* powerHOUSE books, 2005.

Simmons, Annette. *The Story Factor: Inspiration, Influence, and Persuasion Through the Art of Storytelling.* Basic Books, 2000.

Silverman, Lori, editor. *Wake Me Up When the Data is Over: How Organizations Use Stories To Drive Results.* Jossey-Bass, 2006.

Walker, Rob. *Buying In: The Secret Dialogue Between What We Buy and Who We Are.* Random House, 2008.

ABOUT THE AUTHOR

As the President of **Get Storied** (www.getstoried.com) Michael Margolis teaches businesses, nonprofits, and entrepreneurs how to get others to believe in their story.

Michael is a contributing author to the leading compendium on strategic storytelling, *Wake Me Up When The Data is Over: How Organizations Use Stories to Drive Results* (Jossey-Bass, 2006), as well as a contributor to the *Employee Communications Guidebook* (PR News, 2009).

Michael teaches at the business school level as an executive education instructor for the Schulich School of Business in Toronto, Canada, and their Masters in Brand Communications program. He also is a new venture coach and evaluator for the NYU Stern $100K Social Venture Competition.

In 2002, Michael founded **THIRSTY-FISH**, one of the world's first storytelling consultancies working at the intersection of branding, innovation, and organizational change. Michael has worked on many game-changing projects for clients including Ernst & Young, NASA, Marriott, The Nature Conservancy, and YWCA of O'ahu. He's delivered keynotes and workshops around the world to audiences including National Audubon Society, PBS Hawaii, and United Nations Foundation.

Michael began his career as a founding member of two pioneering nonprofits. In 1998, Volunteer Solutions won the M.I.T. $50K Entrepreneurship Competition and later merged with the United Way. His second start-up, CitySkills, was an ambitious market-maker (funded by the Ford and Rockefeller Foundations) that tackled the workforce dimensions of the Digital Divide.

Born in America, Michael grew up in Switzerland before returning to the States in 1986. He's lived in Los Angeles, Boston, Washington D.C., and today calls New York City his home. Michael eats dark chocolate almost every day, and occasionally hosts Willy Wonka-inspired parties. He welcomes your feedback and correspondence at michael@believemethebook.com.

ARE YOU READY TO CREATE A BIGGER STORY?

You can reinvent a more powerful and resonant story faster and easier than you think. It's time to learn how to move beyond your current story's constraints and find a more effective means of large-scale change.

Get Storied helps companies, nonprofits and entrepreneurs get others to believe in their story. **Get Storied** offers a variety of services that teach organizations how to shift perceptions and align people around a common, consistent story. Clients are forward-thinking leaders that must deliver on an ambitious change-agenda connected to vision, brand, and financial engagement goals. Visit www.getstoried.com to learn more.

Get Storied services include:

☐ **INDIVIDUALIZED COACHING** – Receive tailored 1:1 counsel for quick breakthroughs and responsive story refinement, designed especially for small business owners, social entrepreneurs, and visionary executives that want more story mojo.

☐ **KEYNOTES, WORKSHOPS, WEBINARS** – Spice up your conferences, retreats, and in-house events with an inspired and provocative presentation that expands possibilities, and teaches how to turn current and potential supporters into true believers.

☐ **HIGH-STAKES STORYTELLING (Winter 2010)** – Get results with a 6-month executive education program that blends action learning, real-time design, and individualized attention to bring your new, high-stakes story into cultural acceptance.

☐ **CONSULTING** – Strengthen institutional buy-in for major change or innovation with guidance from an experienced, in-the-trenches expert who undestands the demands of organizational transformation.

Michael helped us find our way back to being relevant to today's women.

The journey was engaging, collaborative, and truly transformational. We have finally overcome the roadblocks that stood in the way of renewed engagement.

Our membership, donation levels, and participation are increasing in dramatic ways!

—CHERYL KAUHANE LUPENUI, CEO
YWCA of O'ahu, Hawaii's Largest Women's Organization

SPECIAL BONUSES

As a "thank you" for purchasing BELIEVE ME, you're entitled to receive these FREE resources now from author Michael Margolis:

1. Story Engagement Index. Use this quick self-assessment to see how your current story measures up, and where you might find places you can strengthen your story's engagement factor.

2. BELIEVE-ME **Action Guide.** Discover the essential building blocks of business storytelling that **Get Storied** programs and client successes are built on—a timeless resource for any change-maker or innovator.

3. Subscription to Michael's *Story Mojo* newsletter. Get an insider's perspective on what it *really* takes to reinvent your story: relevant resources and thought-provoking insights on the business storytelling process.

4. BELIEVE ME **Strategy Session.** Whether you're planning a full-scale initiative or simply seeking one-on-one help to improve your existing story, you'll leave the free call clear and excited about what's really possible and practical.

To collect your free resources simply visit
www.believemethebook.com/bonus

Contact Michael at:
michael@getstoried.com
212-777-0813
www.getstoried.com

To order additional copies of BELIEVE ME **or take advantage of bulk discounts for 10 or more copies, please visit** www.believemethebook.com.

3839105

Made in the USA